CHANGE & RESILIENCE

by

Holly Duhig

CRABTREE
PUBLISHING COMPANY
WWW.CRABTREEBOOKS.COM

CRABTREE
PUBLISHING COMPANY
WWW.CRABTREEBOOKS.COM

**Published
in Canada
Crabtree Publishing**
616 Welland Avenue
St. Catharines, ON
L2M 5V6

**Published in
the United States
Crabtree Publishing**
PMB 59051
350 Fifth Ave, 59th Floor
New York, NY 10118

Published in 2019 by Crabtree Publishing Company

First Published by Book Life in 2018
Copyright © 2018 Book Life

Author: Holly Duhig

Editors: Madeline Tyler, Janine Deschenes

Design: Danielle Rippengill

Proofreader: Melissa Boyce

Print and production coordinator:
  Katherine Berti

Printed in the U.S.A./122018/CG20181005

Photographs
Shutterstock
    Denis Makarenko: p. 29 (center left)
    Everett Collection: p. 29 (center right)
    fitzcrittle: p. 16
    Gerry Justice: p. 17
    Jerome460: p. 15
    Kathy Hutchins: p. 20
    Nicolas Economou: p. 14
    punghi: p. 22 (bottom right)
    Twin Design: p. 6 (center right)
Wikimedia Commons
    ONU Brasil (www.youtube.com/watch?v=Z3WmCUnDRJ4)
      p. 23
    United Nations (www.youtube.com/watch?v=Z3WmCUnDRJ4)
      p. 22 (center right)
All other images by Shutterstock

Library and Archives Canada Cataloguing in Publication

Duhig, Holly, author
        Change and resilience / Holly Duhig.

(Our values)
Includes index.
Issued in print and electronic formats.
ISBN 978-0-7787-5433-6 (hardcover).--
ISBN 978-0-7787-5496-1 (softcover).--ISBN 978-1-4271-2224-7 (HTML)

        1. Resilience (Personality trait) in children--Juvenile literature.
2. Resilience (Personality trait)--Juvenile literature. 3. Adaptability
(Psychology) in children--Juvenile literature. 4. Adaptability
(Psychology)--Juvenile literature. 5. Adjustment (Psychology) in
children--Juvenile literature. 6. Adjustment (Psychology)--Juvenile
literature. I. Title.

BF723.R46D84 2018   j155.4′1824   C2018-905497-2
                                            C2018-905498-0

Library of Congress Cataloging-in-Publication Data

Names: Duhig, Holly, author.
Title: Change and resilience / Holly Duhig.
Description: New York : Crabtree Publishing Company, [2018] |
  Series: Our values | Includes index.
Identifiers: LCCN 2018043791 (print) | LCCN 2018045852 (ebook) |
  ISBN 9781427122247 (Electronic) |
  ISBN 9780778754336 (hardcover) |
  ISBN 9780778754961 (pbk.)
Subjects: LCSH: Adjustment (Psychology) in children--Juvenile literature. |
  Resilience (Personality trait) in children--Juvenile literature. |
  Change--Juvenile literature. | Social change--Juvenile literature. |
  Change (Psychology)--Juvenile literature.
Classification: LCC BF723.A28 (ebook) | LCC BF723.A28 D84 2018 (print) |
  DDC 155.4/1824--dc23
LC record available at https://lccn.loc.gov/2018043791

CONTENTS

Words that are **boldfaced** can be found in the glossary on page 31.

WHAT IS CHANGE?

Change is the word we use when things become different from the way they were before. Change is a normal part of life. People, circumstances, and beliefs change. As time passes, our lives change. Changes can be positive, negative, or a mix of both. Imagine you are moving to a new neighborhood. This is a huge change to go through! A good result of this change might be that you make a new friend in your new neighborhood. A negative result might be having to leave your old hockey team.

MEETING NEW FRIENDS IS A GOOD KIND OF CHANGE.

Most of the time, change is a mixture of both good and bad outcomes. It is normal to be worried about changes happening in our lives and our circumstances. However, it is also important to be prepared for changes and to develop skills and qualities that can help you deal with them in positive ways. Being **optimistic** can help you focus on the good things. Learning problem-solving skills can help you work through the challenges that arise when change happens. Having **grit** helps you overcome obstacles.

Often, changes get easier as we grow older. Most older people have experienced many changes throughout their lifetime. They have seen new governments **elected**, new technology invented, and new family members born and grow up. They might even have lived through wars and seen the borders of countries change. For many of them, these kinds of changes feel normal.

YOU CAN LEARN A LOT FROM PEOPLE WHO HAVE LIVED THROUGH MANY CHANGES. ASK A GRANDPARENT, OR OLDER RELATIVE OR COMMUNITY MEMBER, ABOUT THE BIG CHANGES THEY HAVE SEEN IN THEIR LIFETIME.

For young people, changes might feel sudden and unexpected. It can often feel like changes happen to you or around you without your control. For example, your parents might decide to move to a new community. As a young person, you are not in control of this decision and it can feel very unfair. It is important to talk about these feelings to adults in your life because they can help you understand why changes are happening. Changes are sometimes out of adults' control too, even though it seems like they are the ones making the decisions. For example, you might need to move because one of your parents has acquired a new job. This is something that's not in their control.

CHANGE AROUND US

Change is all around us and can happen in any part of our lives. It can be a personal change that affects only you. Larger changes might affect your whole family or community. Even bigger changes are worldwide. It's important to be aware of global changes as well as those that are personal to us. We are all part of a global community. All of the people who share planet Earth are connected in this community. Change in one part of the world can affect others in the global community, too. For example, conflict in some parts of the world can cause refugees to flee their homes to seek shelter in new countries. This affects all people on Earth.

SOCIAL MEDIA CAN PROVIDE A WAY FOR PEOPLE TO GET THEIR STORIES OUT THERE AND GATHER SUPPORT FOR POSITIVE CHANGE.

SOCIAL CHANGE

When the makeup or order of a society is altered, or becomes different, we call this social change. These changes might be in how people think or act as a group. Change can happen on small and large scales. In recent years, the Internet and social media have allowed social change to spread throughout the world quickly. The Internet can be an important tool for positive social change. It is sometimes used to gather support and organize demonstrations or protests that call for social change. For example, the National School Walkout in the United States in March 2018 was organized online. It called for stricter gun laws after 17 students were killed in a school shooting in February of that year. Social media campaigns, such as #WeNeedDiverseBooks, also raise awareness about issues and gather support for social causes.

POLITICAL CHANGE

Changes in governments are known as political changes. Governments are groups of people who control countries, states and provinces, and communities. Political changes are often complex. Usually, people view political changes in different ways, depending on their perspective. People have different political views—sometimes extreme ones. What some perceive as a good political change might be perceived as negative to others.

IN MANY COUNTRIES, VOTING IS A RIGHT THAT ALLOWS PEOPLE TO AFFECT, OR BE PART OF, POLITICAL CHANGES. YOU CAN VOTE FOR CHANGES IN WHO REPRESENTS YOU IN GOVERNMENT. IN THE UNITED STATES AND CANADA, CITIZENS MUST BE 18 YEARS OLD OR OLDER TO VOTE.

Political changes can affect many people on Earth. Political leaders and parties have different goals and objectives. They might create laws to meet their goals. These affect all the people in their country, or even people in other countries. As new governments and leaders are elected or take power undemocratically, new global alliances and agreements are made. Trade between countries might be affected. Wars could be started or ended. **Oppression** could begin, end, or worsen. That's why it's important to stay informed about political changes—even if they are in a different country from your own.

PERSONAL CHANGES

Some changes are personal to you and your life. Graduating from elementary, middle, or high school is one example of a change in your personal circumstances. Other examples might include having a new teacher, experiencing **puberty**, and meeting new friends. Many personal changes are common to a lot of people. They are often important stepping stones that help you learn as you grow older. Most youths graduate from an elementary or middle school before attending high school. When you change schools, your position changes. You might go from being a leader in your elementary school to being one of the youngest students at your new school. This kind of change might affect how you see yourself. You might have different responsibilities at a new school or play a different role in your school community. Learning to work through big changes is an important part of growing up.

MAKING FRIENDS WITH AN OLDER STUDENT WHO CAN SHOW YOU AROUND MAY MAKE THE TRANSITION INTO HIGH SCHOOL EASIER.

CHANGES AT HOME

Personal changes might also include changes in our family circumstances. All families are different and they are always growing and changing. Sometimes this change can feel overwhelming but, over time, changes become the new normal. For example, many youths live with parents who have separated or **divorced**. They might live with one parent for half the time and another parent for the other half. Other youths live with extended family or foster families. Big changes happen in families when births and deaths of loved ones occur. When family situations change, it can feel uncertain, sad, or frightening. It is OK to feel all kinds of emotions when our home lives change. Talking about how we feel can help us come to terms with change.

ALL OF YOUR RELATIONSHIPS SHOULD BE HEALTHY AND POSITIVE PARTS OF YOUR LIFE. IF THEY ARE NOT, YOU MIGHT NEED TO MAKE A CHANGE.

Other personal changes might involve friends or romantic relationships. Our relationships with others change as we grow older. It is normal for friends to grow apart or for romantic relationships to end. Changes like this can be challenging, too! Much of how we see ourselves comes from how we relate to others. When relationships change, we might see ourselves in different ways.

9

WHAT IS RESILIENCE?

Resilience is the ability to **cope** with the changes, challenges, and setbacks that you may come across in your life. It means that not only can you overcome challenges—you can learn from them and grow more resilient in the future. Resilience, like confidence or courage, is a personal **characteristic** that can be built and used to overcome challenges. There are many steps you can take to be more resilient. Some of them are below.

Be aware
Notice the types of changes that are going on in your personal life and in the world around you.

Think Critically
Think critically about the changes that you face. This means that you think about the perspectives of everyone involved and understand that there may be more to learn.

Draw on Past Experiences
When you face new challenges, reflect on past experiences of overcoming challenges. Talk to peers or family members who may have experienced something similar.

Ask for Help
Asking for help is an important part of being resilient. Nobody should be expected to cope with difficult change alone.

THE WORD RESILIENCE COMES FROM THE LATIN WORD "RESILIENS," MEANING "TO REBOUND." THIS IS WHY PEOPLE OFTEN TALK ABOUT "BOUNCING BACK" FROM DIFFICULT SITUATIONS.

WE SHOULD BE AWARE OF CHANGES IN OUR THOUGHTS AND FEELINGS AS WELL AS IN THE WORLD AROUND US.

BEING SELF-AWARE

As well as being aware of change in the wider world, resilience also involves being aware of your own thoughts and emotions and the way you react to change or challenges. Do you have a **growth mindset**, in which you believe that you can overcome challenges, learn from mistakes, and achieve your goals with hard work? Having this mindset can help you overcome difficult changes or challenges. For example, if you have a test

coming up at school, do you feel as if you won't succeed? Being a little nervous is normal, but if we believe we won't succeed we are likely to lose confidence. It's important to be aware of how our thoughts might affect us. Is it true that you won't succeed on the test, or can you think of a time you did well on a test, and prove this thought wrong? Being able to recognize and healthily manage negative thoughts and emotions are part of being resilient.

BUILDING RESILIENCE

Resilience is a character trait that can take time to develop. It requires you to have a positive growth mindset and to work on skills and qualities that will help you be resilient, no matter what comes your way. Some of the skills and qualities that help build resilience are below.

CONFIDENCE

Confidence means that you believe in and rely on yourself. Having confidence means we know we are capable of overcoming challenges and difficult changes. This quality is like a muscle—we need to exercise it to keep it strong. Doing more of the things that you are good at is one way to build confidence. You can also build confidence by trying new things—especially things that might make you feel **apprehensive**. Speaking up in class, volunteering to lead a project, or simply telling a joke to our friends can help us feel confident and realize we can do things we may previously have been too shy to try.

BUILDING CONFIDENCE CAN ALSO HELP YOU DEVELOP STRONGER SELF-ESTEEM. THIS IS THE DEGREE TO WHICH YOU SEE YOURSELF IN A POSITIVE LIGHT.

OPTIMISM

This quality means that you can focus on the positive aspects of challenges, changes, and issues. An optimistic person faces the things that challenge them with positivity and hope. They identify the parts of the challenge that they know they can overcome. Or, they focus on the outcomes of a change that they know or hope will be positive. They do not allow negative thoughts to take control of how they see something.

TAKING RESPONSIBILITY

Another way that resilience can be built up is through taking responsibility. With change often comes new or different responsibilities, or things you are expected to do. For example, when you start high school, your teachers will expect you to complete more work. Taking responsibility means that you stay organized, and complete what is expected of you. By taking responsibility, you are staying in control of how you adapt to change. Taking responsibility keeps you resilient because it helps you meet changes head on.

One strategy that helps build responsibility is learning time management skills. These help you plan your tasks so that you can meet your goals and complete those things, such as homework, for which you are responsible. Focusing on setting and reaching goals by taking responsibility and managing time can help you become more resilient.

GRIT AND PROBLEM SOLVING

Grit is a mindset that involves the qualities of persistence and determination. These qualities mean that you do not give up when you meet challenges. People with grit finish what they start and they work hard to overcome the obstacles they face. To be resilient, we need to have grit. Related to grit are problem-solving skills. These involve being able to approach a problem with an open mind, and trying different solutions until finding one that works. Everyone can build grit and problem-solving skills by persevering and learning from mistakes and failures. This can help you be resilient in times of challenge and change.

DEALING WITH GLOBAL CHANGE

With all of the serious global changes happening around us, it can feel difficult to be resilient. We may feel that we have no contol over the difficult or bad things happening in the world. It is easy to become **apathetic** and feel as though there is nothing you can do. However, staying resilient as a global community can help us overcome big changes, and help those in need. Sometimes, changes mean that whole countries, and millions of people, are affected by things such as war, poverty, or natural disasters. Many political changes also negatively affect huge numbers of people. Part of being resilient is being able to hope for a better future.

Refugee crises have been some of the largest and most upsetting changes on the world stage in the past few years. In recent years, **civil war** in Syria has caused around five million people to flee the country. Over 6.5 million people are **internally displaced** within Syria. Even more people from other countries affected by war, such as Iraq, Afghanistan, and Eritrea in East Africa, also had to flee their homes.

THE JOURNEYS REFUGEES TAKE FROM THEIR HOME COUNTRIES TO SAFETY ARE USUALLY LIFE-THREATENING. MANY REFUGEES FROM SYRIA WERE FORCED TO TRAVEL ON UNSAFE AND OVERCROWDED BOATS TO REACH EUROPE. MANY DIED ON THE JOURNEY.

Refugees who flee their homes seek **asylum** in new countries. They need governments of other countries to agree to give them safety and offer them assistance. They usually wait in refugee camps for long periods—sometimes years—before being accepted to a new country. Many are not accepted at all. Some countries are unwilling to do so. However, refugees rely on others in the global community to help them survive. Even if they do survive their journeys and find new homes, they have undergone extremely traumatic changes. They need a lot of support to adapt to their new lives and heal from the violence they have endured.

REFUGEES WELCOME

HIAS Welcome the stranger. Protect the refugee.

#JewsForRefugees

PLE WERE GEES TOO

AROUND THE WORLD, PROTESTERS SHOWED RESILIENCE BY WORKING TO WELCOME AND SUPPORT REFUGEES.

We can work through the bad changes happening around the world by making an effort to be a force of positive change. Many people work to assist refugees by donating clothes, food, and money. Some people welcome refugees to their new homes and help them get settled. Others volunteer in refugee camps all over Europe to help keep refugees safe and healthy while they are stranded. Many people also put pressure on their governments to provide asylum to more refugees.

AN ACTIVE PART OF CHANGE

When personal and global changes out of our control affect our lives, we might feel frustrated or overwhelmed. It is normal to feel as though it is too difficult or challenging to make a difference. However, there are some ways that we can affect, or create, positive change in the world around us.

A small-scale way that we can be an active part of change in the world is to affect small, personal changes with the people around us. We can treat people with kindness and respect each day, and make a positive difference in their lives. By treating others with respect, you might influence them to do the same, and create positive change in their community, too.

THESE VOLUNTEERS ARE PARTICIPATING IN A RUN TO RAISE MONEY AND AWARENESS FOR BREAST CANCER RESEARCH.

Volunteering is a way that you can create positive change in your community and in the wider world. To volunteer is to spend your time working for a cause, without pay.

Volunteering can include anything from helping raise money to support people living in refugee camps, to giving up your time to help organize a charity event at your school or in your local area.

Activism is taking action to push for change. There are many ways of getting involved in activism. You could write a letter to your government representative asking them to take action on an issue that you feel strongly about, or asking them to change a law that affects you. You could also write a letter to a local newspaper to ask for change and get your opinion heard. Some people write open letters about issues they would like to change, and share it on social media in order to stand up for positive change. You could also sign a **petition** that calls for change on an issue.

Protests and demonstrations are another kind of activism. These are when groups of people organize to raise attention about a certain issue and demand change from those in power—usually members of government or business leaders. These people are demonstrating to show their support of Medicaid in the United States, a program that helps some people with health-care costs.

Yet another kind of activism is boycotting. This is when people refuse to buy or use certain products and services as a form of protest. Sometimes, the business practices of large companies are unethical. Boycotting is a great way of standing up to these unethical practices and demanding change.

After an oil spill in the Gulf of Mexico caused large-scale damage to the environment, many people boycotted big oil companies. Another example of boycotting might be refusing to buy products from cosmetics or hygiene companies that test on animals.

RESILIENCE AND NEWS MEDIA

Part of being resilient to change is being aware of the changes happening in the world around you. One way that we get information about the world around us is through the media. In the past, people mainly used traditional media sources, such as television and newspapers, to learn about the changes in the world around them. Today, most people read and watch much of the news online and on social media. In fact, recent studies have shown that more than half of people in North America get at least some of their news online, including through social media.

There is so much information available online that it can be difficult to sift through it to find reliable information about global events. Since anyone can post information online, there can be **misinformation** in some online news. You may have heard the phrase "fake news" used to describe this. Fake news stories are stories that aren't true. Some stories are completely made up and have been written by people wanting to make money from clicks and shares. Other news stories have some truth to them but contain misinformation, or have been written by someone who has exaggerated or misrepresented facts to influence you to see something from their perspective only.

ONLINE ARTICLES WITH SHOCKING OR TOO-GOOD-TO-BE-TRUE HEADLINES ARE CALLED CLICKBAIT ARTICLES.

Because fake news can be shared by anyone, it is often difficult to tell it apart from real news. Part of being resilient in today's world is learning some **media literacy** skills that can help you seek out credible information and spot fake news when you encounter it.

A CRITICAL LOOK

When you search for news online, or hear and view it on your radio or television, use some of these critical thinking questions to evaluate the stories and accurately get information about changes in the world around you.

- Do you know and trust the organization that published or broadcasted the article? Are they well-known and credible? If the story is written, who is the author? Are they qualified to write about that topic, either through experience or education?

- Does the story sound believable? Often, if something sounds too shocking or too good to be true, it is not real.
- Does the headline match the information in the story?
- Have you heard the story anywhere else in the media?
- If the source is online, check the web address. Does it raise any red flags? Sometimes fake news websites imitate the addresses of legitimate news sources.

RESILIENCE, SELF-ESTEEM, AND MEDIA

Unfortunately, news is not the only thing that is misrepresented in the media. We also see misleading representations of people—which can affect how we view ourselves. By commonly presenting a certain image of male or female beauty, the media has created a **normalized** image of how people should look, or aspire to look. This look is called "conventional beauty." However, images of people are often heavily edited to make them fit this standard of beauty. They do not represent how most people look. Similarly, media that features only a "normalized" view of beauty does not reflect the diversity in our society. When we don't see ourselves reflected in the media we consume, we might feel that we don't fit in with what is beautiful or normal. There is a lot of pressure to fit in with media standards and it can be difficult to stay resilient.

TAKE A LOOK AT THE **CAST** OF THE POPULAR DISNEY SHOW *ANDI MACK*. DO YOU FEEL THE CAST REPRESENTS THE DIVERSITY OF OUR WORLD? WHY OR WHY NOT?

BEING RESILIENT HELPS US TO NOT LET THE MEDIA AFFECT OUR SELF-ESTEEM IN A NEGATIVE WAY. IT MEANS WE RECOGNIZE THAT ALL PEOPLE ARE DIFFERENT AND VALUABLE IN THEIR OWN WAY—DESPITE WHAT SOME MEDIA TELLS US.

We can stay resilient in the face of media pressure by thinking critically about the messages that the media sends about how people look. Ask yourself whether certain images are used to sell a product. Unrealistic images might be used to make viewers feel as though they need to buy a product to look more like the people they see in the advertisement. Recognizing when images are used in this way can help you realize that they are not true reflections of how people should look. Similarly, entertainment media might feature "conventionally beautiful" actors in order to gain a larger audience. Make sure you also think critically about the social media you consume. When you view social media, remember that usually you are seeing the best parts of others' lives. Research has found that Facebook users tend to believe that other users are happier and more successful than they are. Many people also follow the lives of influencers or vloggers on YouTube or Instagram. Remember that usually they are being paid by sponsors to present a certain image. You may not be seeing the reality of their day-to-day lives. By maintaining a critical eye as a media consumer, you can build resilience to media pressures to look or act a certain way.

A RESILIENCE CASE STUDY

Learning about the stories of brave, resilient youths around the world can help us be resilient, too. As you read Yusra Mardini's story, think about why it was important for her to stay resilient in the face of extreme danger. How did she overcome the difficult changes and challenges she faced?

When 17-year-old Yusra Mardini was living in her hometown of Damascus, Syria, she was an ordinary teen who went to school, hung out with friends, and trained in swimming.

When the civil war broke out in 2011, her city quickly became more dangerous. The pool where she trained as a swimmer was bombed. Yusra and her sister were forced to flee Syria. (Her father had previously left to find work, and her mother and younger sister followed later.) They traveled through Lebanon and into Turkey in an effort to reach Greece by boat. They had to sleep in a forest for four nights before getting on a boat to cross the Mediterranean Sea.

The sisters were only 20 minutes into their journey when the boat's motor stopped. The overcrowded boat was close to **capsizing** and most people on board could not swim.

YUSRA MARDINI

THE BOAT YUSRA WAS ON WAS MEANT FOR SIX PEOPLE, BUT CARRIED 20.

Showing extreme courage, Yusra, her sister, and a couple of other strong swimmers immediately jumped into the water to stop the boat from sinking. Yusra swam, towing the boat with a rope for three-and-a-half hours without giving up. She was very scared but a six-year-old boy, Mustafa, whom they'd met on their journey, motivated her to keep going. Although she was terrified, she displayed perseverance and determination—helping to save the lives of all of the refugees on board. Eventually, the sisters reached Germany and were reunited with their family.

YUSRA IS NOW TRAINING FOR THE 2020 OLYMPICS IN TOKYO.

DESPITE HER TRAUMATIC EXPERIENCE, IT WAS ONLY A WEEK BEFORE YUSRA SWAM IN **OPEN WATER** AGAIN.

Just one year later, Yusra competed at the Olympic Games in Rio de Janeiro, Brazil, as part of the first-ever refugee team. This was a team made up of ten talented and resilient athletes who were also refugees from different countries. Yusra and and her sister have also won awards for their bravery. Yusra is still campaigning for change. She is now a **UNHCR** Goodwill Ambassador, and has met with former U.S. president Barack Obama, and Pope Francis. She advocates for the safety of other refugees around the world and works to stop the discrimination that refugees sometimes face. She also speaks to world leaders about her experience, to ask them to support refugees.

RESILIENCE AND DECISION MAKING

Part of developing resilience is learning to make positive decisions that benefit your personal growth. To make positive decisions, you need to be able to **analyze** your decision-making process and the way you usually respond to changes. Many decisions that people make are motivated either by fear or by a desire to grow or change. Imagine a person who fears public speaking trying to decide whether to take part in a school play. They know that performing in front of many people can be a frightening experience. However, taking a chance on the play might result in a positive outcome. They might find that facing their fear helps them grow as a person—they might get better at public speaking or become more confident. In this case, choosing to take part in the play is a decision motivated by personal growth. Not taking part is a decision motivated by fear.

THINK BACK TO SOME OF THE DECISIONS YOU HAVE MADE IN YOUR LIFE. WERE THEY MOTIVATED BY FEAR OR GROWTH?

VISUALIZATION

It can be difficult to make decisions at times because we are scared of what could go wrong. We might imagine the possible negative outcomes of our decisions. However, it is possible to change the way we think about decisions, to help us become more resilient when it comes to making difficult decisons. We can do so with visualization, a strategy that involves imagining and focusing on the positive outcomes of a decision. The more you can visualize the positive outcomes, the more motivated you might be to achieve those outcomes—and the more likely you are to make them happen.

VISUALIZATION CAN BE A POWERFUL TOOL. CLOSING YOUR EYES AND LISTENING TO MUSIC CAN HELP WITH VISUALIZATION.

REFLECTION

Reflection is a helpful strategy that you can use to develop positive decision-making skills long-term. Each time you make a big decision, such as deciding whether to participate in a school play, reflect on the outcomes of your decision. It could be useful to create a chart or mind map of the positive and negative outcomes that took place. Ask yourself whether you might make a different decision next time. Think critically about what motivated the decision you made and whether a different decision might have pushed your personal growth and helped build your resilience.

25

YOUR RESILIENCE TOOLKIT

You now know how important resilience is in dealing with the many changes and challenges you face every day. Moving forward, you can develop a "toolkit" of strategies to help you continue to develop and use resilience in your life. Below are some strategies that could be part of a resilience toolkit. Try each strategy and decide which work best for you. Then, keep the strategies you like in your own "resilience toolkit"!

APPROACH CHANGE WITH POSITIVITY

When things change, it is important to remember that we can choose to focus on the positive outcomes change may bring. Change can bring new experiences, new friends, and new challenges that will make you a stronger person. When you are nervous about change, it can help to look back at past experiences where change has been positive. Visualize the positive outcomes you hope will happen and use optimism to focus on them. How you approach individual changes can improve your view on change in general—and help you develop resilience.

CAN YOU THINK OF A TIME THAT A CHANGE IN YOUR LIFE BROUGHT A POSITIVE OUTCOME?

PRIORITIZE SELF-CARE

To be resilient, you need to take care of yourself. You need to be healthy and in a good state of mind to make positive decisions, stay optimistic, and work on the qualities, such as grit, that help you build resilience. Make sure you get enough sleep and food that is good for you. If you are feeling stressed or unwell, take time for self-care until you feel better. Self-care is different for different people. It might involve doing something you love, taking time to relax, or talking about how you feel with a trusted friend.

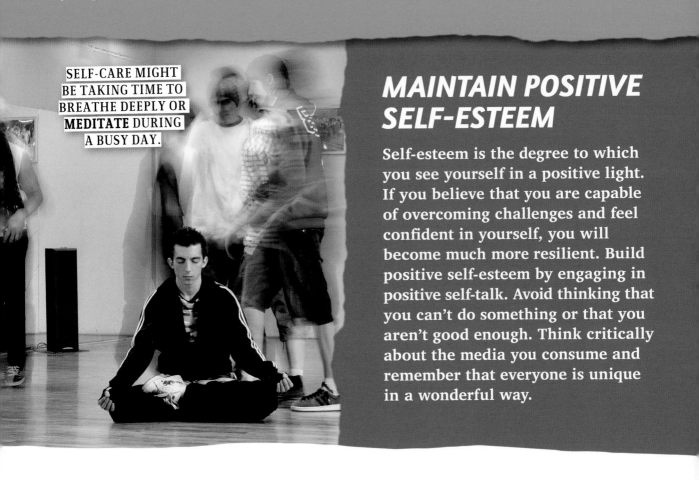

SELF-CARE MIGHT BE TAKING TIME TO BREATHE DEEPLY OR **MEDITATE** DURING A BUSY DAY.

MAINTAIN POSITIVE SELF-ESTEEM

Self-esteem is the degree to which you see yourself in a positive light. If you believe that you are capable of overcoming challenges and feel confident in yourself, you will become much more resilient. Build positive self-esteem by engaging in positive self-talk. Avoid thinking that you can't do something or that you aren't good enough. Think critically about the media you consume and remember that everyone is unique in a wonderful way.

KEEP A ROUTINE

A routine is made up of regular daily activities that you do at a similar time each day. They might include going to bed at the same time each night or eating a **nutritious** breakfast in the morning. Routines can help you deal with big changes because they maintain some normalcy in your day-to-day life. For example, a move is a big change many youths experience. It can be hard to cope with a new home, school, and neighborhood. By maintaining a regular routine, you can keep those parts of your daily life the same even if you are going through a big change.

SET AND WORK TOWARD GOALS

Setting goals is an effective way to build resilience. Goals can be short-term, such as getting a good grade on a school assignment, or long-term, such as becoming a writer one day. Goals help you to focus on the bigger picture—they are a way that you can keep your mind away from smaller changes and setbacks. If you face a challenge or change, focus on your longer-term goals and how you will reach them. When you experience a setback, it does not mean you will not reach your goals. Being able to overcome the setbacks is the most important lesson. Small steps will help you reach goals, and allow you to build resilience along the way!

BY BEING KIND AND SUPPORTIVE, YOU CAN BE PART OF SOMEONE ELSE'S SUPPORT NETWORK, TOO. HELPING OTHERS MIGHT ALSO MAKE YOU FEEL MORE CONFIDENT IN YOUR ABILITIES, HELPING YOU TO TACKLE CHALLENGES AND CHANGES.

BUILD A SUPPORT NETWORK

Having a support network means surrounding yourself with people who can help you during times of transition and change. We need others to guide us, give us advice, and support us when we experience negative outcomes of change. Having a strong support network could encourage us to take more chances and embrace more changes, because we know that we have people to help us if the outcomes are not what we hoped. Friends and family, as well as professionals such as teachers, doctors, and even **counselors**, can all be part of your support network.

LOOK TO ROLE MODELS

Being resilient is much easier when you have someone to look up to. Hearing and reading about the stories of people who used resilience to overcome difficult challenges and changes, such as Yusra Mardini, can help us learn strategies to build resilience. Role models can be famous people, or people in our own lives.

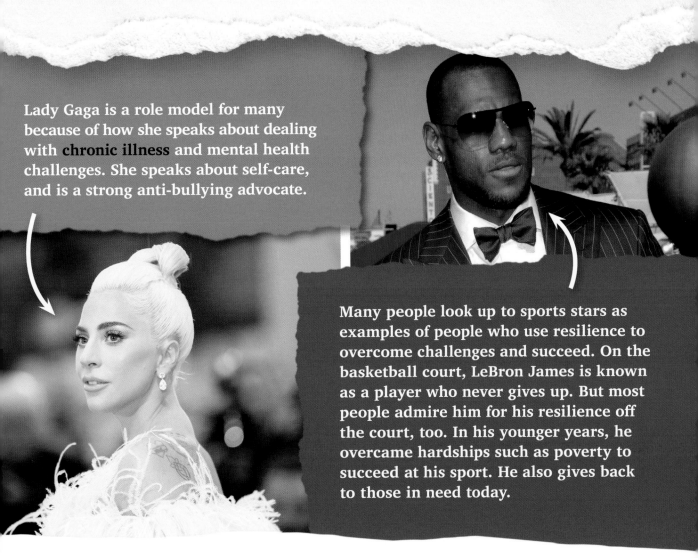

Lady Gaga is a role model for many because of how she speaks about dealing with **chronic illness** and mental health challenges. She speaks about self-care, and is a strong anti-bullying advocate.

Many people look up to sports stars as examples of people who use resilience to overcome challenges and succeed. On the basketball court, LeBron James is known as a player who never gives up. But most people admire him for his resilience off the court, too. In his younger years, he overcame hardships such as poverty to succeed at his sport. He also gives back to those in need today.

GET INVOLVED

Remember that not all changes are out of your control. You can respond to change and even influence positive changes in the future. If change is happening with which you are uncomfortable or disagree, you can speak out about it by protesting, signing petitions, or posting your ideas online. You can also talk to trusted adults to help you. You can be a force for positive change. You can volunteer or take part in activism to campaign for issues you care about and make the world a more positive place.

THINK ABOUT IT

1 Think of a change in your personal life that affected you in some way. What were the outcomes of that change? How did you cope with the change and overcome any challenges that came with it? Did you use any strategies in this book, or strategies of your own?

2 Think about a time you, or someone you know, had to be resilient. What qualities made you, or that person, resilient? Make a list of the qualities and share it with a classmate. Talk about the qualities that you each feel you could work harder to develop, so that you become more resilient in the future.

3 Review the Resilience Toolkit on pages 26 to 29. Then, create your own personal resilience toolkit, with strategies and ideas that you feel would work best for you. Add some of the strategies from this book. Can you think of any new ideas you would add to your personal resilience toolkit? Compare your toolkit with a peer or classmate for more ideas. Then, put it into action the next time you experience a challenge or change.

GLOSSARY

analyze Examine in detail and think critically about

apathetic Showing or feeling no interest, enthusiasm, or concern

apprehensive Fearful or worried that a negative result will occur

asylum Protection given by a country to a refugee

capsizing When a boat is overturning in water

cast The group of actors in a movie, TV show, or play

characteristic One quality of a person that is part of what makes up their identity

chronic illness A long-term or persistent illness, sometimes defined as lasting longer than three months

civil war Fighting between different groups of people in the same country

cope Deal with

counselors People who give advice, especially as a job

divorced When two people who were married legally separate

elected Chose someone to represent them in government

global community All of the people who share planet Earth

grit A mindset in which someone displays perseverance and refuses to give up on their goals

growth mindset A term, coined by Dr. Carol Dweck, that describes the thinking of an individual who believes he or she can develop their abilities and strengths, and add to them over time

headlines The words, called a heading, at the top of an article. A heading tells a reader what they should find in the article.

internally displaced To be forced from your home, but remain in your country

media literacy Being able to identify, analyze, create, and engage with different forms of media

meditate To focus the mind for a period of time, usually to reflect or think carefully about something

misinformation False information

normalized Made something normal, accepted, or standard

nutritious Describes food that contains the substances we need for good health

open water An area of water with no shore in sight

oppression Unjust treatment or persecution that is ongoing

optimistic Describes someone who has a positive view about the future

petition An official written request, usually including many signatures, that asks a person in power to make a change

puberty The period of time in which a person's body matures and becomes able to reproduce, or have babies

sponsors People or organizations who provide money for a project or activity

transition A change

UNHCR Short for the United Nations High Commissioner for Refugees, the UNHCR is a division of the United Nations that focuses on the protection of refugees.

INDEX